EIRA McINTYRE

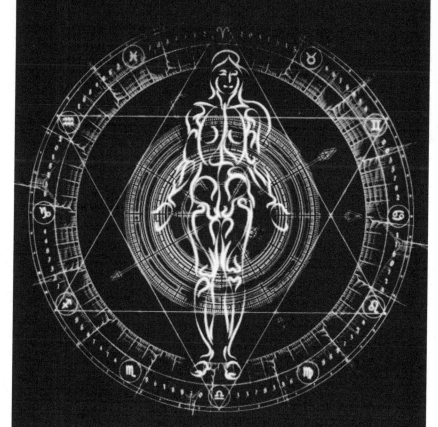

MAGICKAL
REBIRTH

AWAKEN THE WITCH WITHIN &
HARNESS THE POWER OF THE OCCULT

© 2015 Eira McIntyre

This manual is meant for information and educational purposes only. Use it at your own risk. In any case, the author will not be held accountable for any damage or ill effects brought about by the misuse of this guide.

Eira & Her Coven, Celebrating

Eira has been a practicing eclectic pagan for more than two decades, discovering her true path to the Divine at the young age of 19. Beginning as a solitary practitioner for the first fifteen years – self-taught through research and following her instincts –, she was eventually led to a teaching coven in her hometown.

After 5 months with the coven, she became an initiate and coven Scribe. Shortly after that, she began training to become the High Priestess, an honor which she has flourished in for the last five years.

Helping people has been her driving force in life, as part of the coven and in her personal life. Eira married her true love and they have a son together, living happily in New England where they spend their spare time enjoying the four seasons.

Aside from her accomplishments as a High Priestess, Eira has also enjoyed a successful career in restaurant consulting. Since the birth of her son, she has placed her career on the back burner to focus on family and her coven teachings. Eira is also an accomplished artist and loves to cook feasts for the Sabbats.

Table of Contents

Introduction: Magick 101

Why would anyone want to learn magick to begin with? **What's in it for you?**

If you ever had the feeling that your life is missing something, a lack of connection or spirituality, then this book was written for you. Perhaps you already lead a deep spiritual existence but you aren't exactly sure how to harness the power you hold inside to help change the world around you? Perhaps you have always felt that you had the means to make a real difference down here but you never knew what you were supposed to do?

If that describes you, keep reading!

My mission in these pages will be to share with you the knowledge I have garnered over twenty years of learning, experimenting, sharing and discovering **the power that lies within each and every one of us**. There are theories, myths even, that great witches are born, not made.

This is a complete fallacy!

The only advantage "heritage witches" have over any of us is that they grew up under the tutelage and nurturing of other witches. They just got a head start if you will; nothing more!

Learning witchcraft, in a way, will be like approaching a second language. At first, you may stumble, tackling the very basics... but, with time, if you stick to it, you will gain experience and increase your awareness of the immense power you possess. You will grow your skills beyond what you thought possible! Becoming a great witch requires commitment, a thirst for knowledge and self-belief.

This book will be the first in a series that will show you how to harness your natural power, following easy steps to:

- Build confidence;

- Delve deeper into your faith;

- Connect with the Divine.

It is the starting point of an incredible journey that will take you down a path to a richer and more fulfilling life. One that will offer you a feeling of connectedness with all living things and, most importantly, with yourself.

Welcome to a world filled with magick!

Defining the Craft: What It Really Means to Be a Witch

Ever since Man became self-aware and realized that he was mortal, he has been on a quest to discover his purpose in life, his true "path." While many found solace in the church and organized religion, there were many others who were looking for more... For a deeper understanding of the forces of Nature. For a closer kinship with their higher power.

As far as I am concerned, it was a search for the tangible. I wanted to be able to touch, feel, and see proof of God's existence. I wanted to take control and go beyond the regular experience most folks contented themselves with.

My journey began with reading everything I could on all the major – and not so prevalent – religions. Judaism, Islam, Buddhism, Hinduism... You name it, I studied it! One day, what started out to be just another stroll through the aisles at my local bookstore, revealed to be a key moment that changed my life forever. As I was looking for another book to quench my thirst for knowledge, I came across a section I had never seen before, which read: "New Age". I began scanning the books and pulled out one that seemed promising.

That marked the beginning of my own magickal rebirth.

When people hear the word "witchcraft" or "witch", images of Halloween costumes and Harry Potter often come to mind. For the more God-fearing souls, perhaps even Satan or other devilish thoughts emerge. And who could blame them? Even the Merriam-Webster dictionary inspires nothing but negative emotions when it comes to their definition:

"Witchcraft (noun, /wich-,kraft/): magical things done by witches; the use of magical powers obtained especially from evil spirits."

C'mon, seriously? This isn't the 17th century anymore!

Thankfully, Wikipedia is here to save the day with a more accurate and palatable definition:

"Witchcraft broadly means the practice of, and belief in, magical skills and abilities that are able to be exercised individually, by designated social groups, or by persons with the necessary esoteric secret knowledge. Witchcraft is a complex concept that varies culturally and societally, therefore it is difficult to define with precision. Witchcraft often occupies a religious, divinatory, or medicinal role, and is often present within societies and groups whose cultural framework includes a magical world view."

While this definition is more to the point when explaining that it cannot be defined with any sort of precision, witchcraft is something that began hundreds of years ago – during the simplest of times, when science was still in its infancy. To tell the entire truth, there is absolutely nothing "New Age" about it. **Witchcraft, or magick, is merely science unexplained**!

You see, science is but the study of the physical and natural world that surrounds us. Theories are tested and proven over time through experimentation. Witchcraft works almost in the same manner, but with a bigger emotional engagement because it is based in faith in a higher power.

To further complicate our task, witchcraft also goes by different names. Most of them spawned because of the negative connotation conveyed by the original word, but some others were needed to denote specific branches of the craft.

For example "pagan" is an umbrella term that all those who practice witchcraft fall under, and which is defined as "those who hold religious beliefs other than those of the main world religions."

No wonder that, with one single word covering such a broad description of beliefs, we had to resort to and create other names – such as Wicca, Shamanism, and Druidism to name a few – to help us further clarify exactly what it is we are talking about.

When one mentions "New Age", it refers to the resurgence of the craft over the last 50-60 years. Whether or not it has actually increased in number, or people are becoming more open about their beliefs, is still up for debate. A common saying you will hear, with regards to those who follow the craft and call themselves witches is: "there are more of us than you think!"

The Rules of Magick

While many attribute the basic "rules" or "commandments" of witchcraft to the New Age founders like Doreen Valiente and Gerald Gardner, be aware that these moral codes have been in existence for centuries. With that being said, I will still use the current terminology posed by the New Age sects to make it easier for you to do further research on your own.

The first commandment is the Rule of Three or the **Threefold Law**.

This law states that **whatever energy you put out into the universe will be returned to you, times three**. Similar to Newton's Third Law of Physics, every action has an equal and opposite reaction, but even more closely related to the Law of Attraction. Whatever type of energy vibrations you emit, you will attract even more of it. Happy people tend to attract more happiness and, conversely, negative people attract more negativity.

This law helps guide witches in their spellcrafting. Knowing that whatever you send out will come back to you keeps a great witch from doing harm to others. This brings us to the other tenet closely followed by most honorable witches, commonly known as the **Wiccan Rede**. Again, it has been around for centuries but, for ease of researching, that's what we will call it here.

Doreen Valiente is credited with writing the Wiccan Rede, which is a beautiful poem, explaining the cycle of the moon, casting of the circle, and the Sabbats. The most important words, which have been around for all of pagan history are:

> *"These eight words the Rede fulfill*
>
> *An ye harm none, do what ye will."*

Simply put: **harm no one and do whatever you want**. This includes all living things, as well as yourself.

One key aspect of the craft is casting spells... and it is very tempting to be led down a path towards the dark side. But with great power comes great responsibility. The Rede reminds us to stay in the light, never to be motivated by revenge. Let Karma do her job when it comes to making sure those who do wrong get their due.

Sacred Texts and the Power of Words

For every religion out there, there is a belief system. Catholicism is deeply rooted in the teachings of the Bible; Judaism has strong beliefs in the Torah, and Islam follows the Koran.

In witchcraft, or paganism, we could argue that no such book exists. But that would not be entirely true. In fact, there are many texts for beginners, as well as for advanced studies. There are even ones for fluffy bunnies (for those who think witchcraft is like the old TV show Charmed.)

However, the only book that you should follow absolutely to the letter is the one you will create yourself – often referred to as a Book of Shadows. **The words you write carry an immense amount of personal power**. You will include things like spells, prayers, findings in meditation, moon cycles, recipes... Really anything you want. It is yours!

Like I said, words have strength. They vibrate on a frequency unique to the word and the feelings they elicit. Whether they are Catholic, Christian, Jewish, Islamic or your own, words have that amazing ability to draw forth the emotions needed to create miracles.

There are countless stories of Catholics who pray for healing. Premature babies who miraculously live long healthy lives; patients cured of terminal cancer, and many more. Words are so powerful, yet we seldom realize it. **Words can be used to heal, and they can be used to harm**.

The one thing that ties all religions together is that they are all just different paths up the same mountain; different means to reach the summit. They are all rooted in love. To be close to the Divine is to be loved, and shared with family, friends, neighbors, your community and the world. Whether your summit is known as Nirvana, Heaven, or Mount Olympus, the end result is the same. **LOVE**.

The Secret Ingredients to Unlocking the Power Inside You

If you were to follow this book to the letter, practicing every exercise, repeating every word in every spell, you would never become a truly great witch without two essential ingredients. And those are: **confidence and intent**.

With these two tools in hand, you will have the key to discover how to change your life forever. Understanding their use is critical to your success. Confidence is not something you wave a wand and obtain, nor is it something you can fake. It is built up over time.

The journey to building confidence is as important as remembering which direction is east when casting spells. It ties directly into our belief. Have you ever listened to a fanatic vehemently defending his faith? That's the power of belief and confidence in knowing what you believe it true. And it gains strength over time.

Think of your first day at school or work. Whether you are an introvert or extrovert, it did not really matter. You probably remained quiet, met a few people, but for the most part kept your head down and did your work.

Athletes, most especially professional ones, must have confidence in their abilities. Have you ever watched an athlete lose their confidence and seen what it does to their game? Goes right into the toilet!

With energy work and spells, it is no different. Confidence comes from practice and experiencing results from the effort put into it. When we begin anything, our confidence is shaky; the same will hold true when you will cast your first circle.

That's OK! Don't beat yourself up if you forgot the exact wording to calling the corners. Don't berate yourself because you lit the candles before the incense (remember the Wiccan Rede?) While there certainly are guidelines to follow and reasons for the ways and order we perform our craft, practice makes perfect.

The definition of intent is simply an intention or purpose, further explained as an aim or plan. However, in energy work, with intent comes emotion. **You cannot cast successful spells without putting feeling, emotions or passion into them**.

Think of the best meal you ever had in your life. Maybe it was your mom's delicious pasta or the signature plate of a chef at a fancy restaurant. The love of cooking, and giving pleasurable nourishment, was put into that meal by the person who prepared it. How about school? What was your favorite subject? I will almost guarantee you received nothing but A's in that class.

When emotion is tied to action, the resulting outcome is often much more significant and carries much more meaning. It is the same for spells and every day magick. Without a strong and clear intent, our magick has no oomph or power. Conversely, every thought has energy but not necessarily intent.

Earlier, when I explained the "Wiccan Rede," I included yourself in the definition because your thoughts have energy and can cause extreme harm. Thoughts are damaging when they are negative and helpful when they are positive. It is impossible to feel poorly when thinking happy thoughts. Now add intent to that.

When it is our intention to feel good and we think about pleasurable things such as our beloved families, the vacation we took last year, our precious cat or dog's reaction when we come home from a long day's work, our child's laughter, and so on... it is a more powerful feeling than just thinking good thoughts, isn't it?

Intent and confidence are as essential to magick as yeast is to bread. Without them, your spells will fall flat, and you will not achieve your goal of becoming a powerful witch. With them, watch your spells rise up to the universe and see your desires manifest through your magick.

Magick Exercise I – Visualize to Grow & Thrive

A key skill to building up intent as well as self-assurance is visualization. Here is a short, step by step exercise for you to practice as many times as you like, choosing different scenarios each time.

By perfecting your visualization skills, you will gain confidence in your spellcrafting. It will also provide a way for you to feel your emotions deeply, thus helping to create intent.

- Sitting comfortably in a quiet environment where you will not be disturbed, close your eyes and turn your attention to your breathing. To the air coming into your lungs and flowing back out through your nose;

- Focus your thoughts on that rhythmic pattern, feeling your chest and stomach rise and fall with each breath;

- Imagine a white light permeating the air, flowing

into you, swirling around your chest, and scooping up any debris;

- Let the debris exit your body as you exhale. A little more coming out at each cycle. Repeat seven to eight times or until all the debris have been cleared;

- Envision your deepest desire in your mind's eye. If it is finding your true love, see yourself smiling, preparing dinner for two, candles lit and soft music playing in the background. Imagine leaving space for them to park in your driveway. What do they smell like? Feel like? Imagine holding them close to you in a tight embrace. You don't need to see their face, just experience all the feelings associated with being in love. Keep repeating these images until you have the feeling securely within your heart;

- Open your eyes and continue feeling the love you conjured.

You can do this exercise with a job you covet, financial stability you desire, or anything else for which your heart longs. Practice this daily until you are able to visualize that particular scenario without needing a quiet space or the light meditation beforehand.

Now that you have a basic understanding of how to harness your natural power, let's begin on our journey...

Chapter I – The Importance of Tools

You wouldn't start building a house without the proper tools, like wood, a drill, nails and so on, now would you? The same goes for forging your house of power. Tools are necessary in witchcraft for one purpose: **to focus our emotions and awareness to the task at hand.**

Each tool has its own representation, association and focus. By using the right tool for the right job, we help boost our confidence and narrow down our intent which leads to success in harnessing our true natural power.

Buying vs Making Your Own

This does not necessarily mean you ought to make a run for the nearest new age store and clean out the shelves! Many of the tools we will be dealing with can be found right in your home, or they can be easily made. Take me for example; about ten years ago, I was walking along a beach in Maine and came across a small piece of driftwood... It was the perfect length for a wand and it even showed a three-pronged end to which I could affix a stone.

I took it home with me, dried it and noted that the time it had spent in the ocean had smoothed out its surface, so I didn't even need to sand it. With my hot glue gun, I secured an amethyst to the end. *Voila*! I had created my beloved wand which I still use to this day!

Minimum cost, maximum return.

Is a wand required? Maybe. In the end, only YOU can tell which tools resonate the most with you. You can start small and add new items along the way, giving you a more diverse choice when creating magick.

Below, I will share with you each major tool, with a quick word on their meaning and how they can help you in spellwork. Then, it will be up to you to decide whether to create, buy or pass on each one of them. Trust your gut.

Chalice & Bowl: the Givers of Life

Representing the Goddess, the female aspect of paganism, the Chalice plays an important role in nourishment, fertility and offerings in your craft. The element it represents is Earth, just like the Goddess. The shape is similar to the womb, which is the giver of all life.

Also a representation of the Goddess, typically used for holding water, the Bowl is a symbol of the womb as well, from which all things are born. It is most commonly used in holding water, salt or other spellcrafting ingredients, and can be found in your kitchen cabinet.

Incense: the Messenger

When burning incense, watch the smoke unfurl and carry through the air. The element associated with incense is, in fact, Air which helps open communication and carry messages to the universe, God and Goddess.

Athame: the Separator

A short, ceremonial knife which represents the God and his strength. Most tools shaped like a phallus are associated with the God, representing his fertility and power. The ceremonial knife is used only to cut energy, not cut physical objects. Its element is Fire, associated with the power of the Sun.

Candles: the Facilitators

A very important tool because not only are they associated with fire, the God and power, but they can be used in spellcraft in many ways. Candles can be used in spells, matching the right color with the intent of the spell, or they can be used in divination by watching the flame.

Wand: the Director

The all-purpose wand is used for directing energy. Associated with the East, and the element of Air, it is used in casting circles or channeling energy to a certain spot.

Bell: the Cleanser

While not a common tool, many witches love using a bell because it is associated with the Divine spirit. It calls the attention of the Divine to you and the work you are doing. Bells can also be used for cleansing or purifying energy. It can be used for invocation or banishment, and can ward off evil energies.

Cauldron: the Indispensable

This multi-purpose tool is one of the first purchases I ever made. I recommend spending a little extra and getting a cast iron one because you can use them for decoration and burning everything from incense to written spells. Moreover, as far as I am concerned, something about the cast iron resonates powerfully with me. I use it in almost every spell I cast and, when not in use, it decorates my altar. Associated with the womb of the Goddess and represents Water, the element of the West.

Pentacle: the Protector

The five pointed star has so much symbolism for witches, but most importantly it represents protection. I keep many of them all around me, on my altar, in my purse, my car and around my neck. The pentacle can be handmade easily with 5 sticks and some thread. If you prefer, you can purchase one as well as they are pretty cheap.

Sword: the Caster of Circles

This is a purely ceremonial item and can be used in place of the athame when casting circles. Used only to cut energy, it is a beautiful and not-so-obviously pagan showpiece to display. Associated with the Sun energies and the element of Fire.

Book of Shadows: the Keeper of Records

This is a very important tool, and simple to put together. It is like a witchcraft journal, which can include anything and everything related to the craft. Spells and their results, recipes, Sabbat celebrations, collections of nature's gifts like feathers or leaves can all be a part of your book of shadows because it is yours to create.

Be sure to use something that you can continuously add to over the years, or even have multiple editions as you grow your powers.

And the most important tool of them all:

<u>You, the powerful witch</u>!

The truth is you can cast spells, harness your natural power... without any of these things. All the tools do is help you focus, bring your subconscious and conscious minds in sync and raise the energy within you. YOU are the conduit to the world of magick. Not your tools.

Your Sacred Space

You are probably thinking, "where am I going to put all this stuff?" Great question!

You need to choose a sacred space, one that is all your own. It could be something as innocuous as a windowsill or as blatant as a table in the corner of a room. It all depends on whether you prefer to keep your beliefs and practices hidden unto only you and with those you choose to share it.

The altar is another important tool every great witch should own. It does not have to be a permanent space, but the critical elements are your tools and whatever items you need for your spellcrafting.

The altar or sacred space is where you will conduct your spellcrafting.

If you want to keep your items and sacred space hidden in plain sight, that is easy. Portable altars are easy to make. All you need to do is have something like a chest, tool box, or even a cardboard box in which to hold all your magickal items.

With that being said, note that the space you choose to do a majority of your magickal work in should preferably stay the same because there is always your own residual energy left in that space.

I can almost always tell where someone's sacred space is because the energy it holds is like a magnet to me. This space can be your kitchen island, the floor of your living room, a hidden corner of your yard, or anywhere you feel comfortable and connected.

It is YOUR space to connect to the Divine, so choose where you will be happiest. There is no right or wrong answer.

Many of your tools can be regular household items too. You can pick a wine glass for your chalice, a bowl from your cabinet, a butter knife as an athame, and many other items to include in your tool chest. This will help keep your magickal workings away from prying eyes.

When choosing a more permanent, out-in-the-open space, be mindful of roommates and family members. You don't want to choose your kid's playroom or take over your roommate's bookshelf.

Create a space that is all your own. For my own altar, I use a wood corner TV stand turned magickal cabinet. It sits in the corner of my living room, out of the way, but always within my sight. I keep it cleansed and decorated for each season.

One note about altars, magickal working spaces and pets. If you have cats and/or dogs, they will be nosy. Especially when you get started doing magickal work. No one knows better than I do, having two cats and a dog, how much of a pain in the butt it can be to have to recast a circle because your cat trotted over and broke the energy barrier!

Keep them out of your space when doing work within a circle. Other than that, I find them to be a wonderful addition to my spellwork. As I write this, my cat Lucy is napping on my altar!

Once you have decided which tools to acquire, whether handmade or purchased, and you have chosen a sacred space, it is critical that you cleanse and consecrate them.

All things carry residual energy, some good, some bad. You never want unknown energy to enter your spellworking. This is an important step that should never be skipped.

To ensure your tools are cleansed thoroughly, you will need to use the four elements: earth, air, fire and water.

Consecrating is a different step, which involved nothing but yourself and the tool.

Magick Exercise II – Cleansing Your Space

Ready for your first cleansing ceremony? Gather the following:

- A white candle - Fire;
- A bowl of water (use bottled or distilled until you learn how to make your own moon water) - Water;
- A small cup of sea salt (any salt will do; I just prefer sea salt for the larger granules) - Earth;
- Incense and holder (a sage stick is perfect, as the herb is the quintessential purifier) - Air

Begin with cleansing the altar or sacred space:

1. Take a pinch of salt and, in a counterclockwise motion, sprinkle it onto the altar/space, and say the words:

"By the power of three times three, all that resides within me,

I ask you, powers of Earth to cleanse this space and banish all energy,

as I claim it for my own, so mote it be";

2. Dip your fingers into the bowl of water, and sprinkle it over the altar/space, and say the words:

"By the power of three times three, all that resides within me,

I ask you, powers of Water to cleanse this space and banish all energy,

as I claim it for my own, so mote it be";

3. Light your candle, preferably with a lighter. If you are using a match, do not blow it out! Just shake it out (blowing out candles is offensive to the element of fire.) Use snuffers, wet fingers, or wave out the flame when extinguishing a flame (note of common sense: Goddess forbid, your home or something in your home catches fire, extinguish it by any means necessary!) With your lit candle, pass it in a counterclockwise motion over the altar/space, and say the words:

"By the power of three times three, all that resides within me,

I ask you, powers of Fire to cleanse this space and banish all energy,

as I claim it for my own, so mote it be";

4. Use your lit candle to light your incense. Once lit, place it in a holder securely and pass over the alter/space in a counterclockwise motion over the altar/space, and say the words:

"By the power of three times three, all that resides within me,

I ask you, powers of Air to cleanse this space and banish all energy,

as I claim it for my own, so mote it be."

And with that, your space is now cleansed.

In witchcraft, moving in a counterclockwise (or *widdershins*) motion banishes, while moving in a clockwise (*deosil*) motion increases or welcomes the energy you are manipulating.

Magick Exercise III – Perform the Consecration

Consecrating your tools is another crucial matter. Some witches like to combine the cleansing and consecration steps together, meaning one ritual for both acts. However, I prefer to keep them separate because it allows me more time to connect with my tools and keeps my focus very singularly on one intent at a time.

Of course, you are welcome to try both and do what feels right to you!

The definition of "consecrate" is to dedicate to a religious or divine purpose, which is exactly what we will be doing with the tools, and literally imbibing them with our energy.

The great thing about tools is they can hold parts of our power which can be used at a later time. Stones and crystals for example are excellent for this, which is why they are often used as amulets and talismans.

To consecrate your tools, you will need your sacred space and your tools. Nothing more.

1. Sit comfortably with your tools within arms reach;
2. Close your eyes and take three deep, slow breaths;
3. Hold the first tool in both hands, getting it attuned to your energy vibrations;
4. Say the following spell:

"In the name of the Old Ones, the Ancients

In the name of the Sun, the Moon and the Stars

By the powers of Earth, Air, Fire and Water

I consecrate this (name of tool) and make it my own

As I will, so mote it be!"

5. Repeat these steps for each and every tool, all while holding the tool in your hands for as long as you feel it takes for the necessary energy to be absorbed into the item.

You have now cleansed and consecrated your tools! Congratulations on this important step in one's initiation.

Be sure to add this, with any variations, into your Book of Shadows.

Chapter II: Getting to Know the Elements

What are the elements? Why is it important to know about them? How can they help you become a great and powerful witch?

These questions and more will be answered in this section so as to give you a better understanding of how to use the elements in your daily magickal life.

Attain a Deeper Understanding of the World

There are four classical elements, basically the building blocks of the universe. Earth, Air, Fire, and Water are essential to witchcraft and seasoned witches know how to harness their energies in rituals and spell casting. The fifth element, Spirit, is also known as "Akasha", which is Sanskrit for "space".

To understand the elements, all you have to do is step out into nature. Take a walk through the woods, and find yourself a small stream or lake.

Have a seat on the cool earth, knowing what you are sitting on is a minuscule fraction of the entire planet. Think of all the things happening in and on the Earth in this moment. The energy can seem palpable.

Feel the breeze gently caress your face, the element of air ever moving and flowing. This soothing element can be violent too. That same caress you feel can turn into a whipping destructive force, tearing down trees and even buildings.

As the air dances across your face, the sun shines his rays upon you, warming not only your skin, but your heart also.

Sun, the ultimate symbol of fire, symbolizes transformation. A pile of wood is just wood until you add the element of fire, transforming the wood into smoke, embers and ash.

Dip your toes into the stream or lake, feel the soothing water flow over your feet. The element of water is a cleansing one, washing away dirt as well as negativity and obstacles. You are made of water, and it is one of the essential elements to all living things.

Spirit can be found in all the elements, just as all the elements can be found in the Spirit. It is the essence of the divine, the element that binds us all together.

Close your eyes and imagine a wisp of energy flowing through and connecting all living things around you, including yourself. This is Spirit, the divine spark that resides within us all.

To understand the four classical elements, it is best to experience them with all your senses – touch, taste, sight, sound, and smell – as they will evoke different emotions within you.

The emotion you feel is the Spirit, the god and goddess speaking to you through the elements.

Once you reach understanding of each, you are ready to

begin working with them. They are powerful tools in the Craft, so use them wisely!

Each one has its own personality, and many of the tools we work with represent an element. Astrology also has its basis in the elements; oftentimes, the characteristics of the element are attributed to the person born under specific signs.

For example, Sagittarius is a fire sign and people born under it are often described as flighty or fickle, often changing just for the sake of change. This is similar to the behavior of a fire burning, the flames ever moving and shifting.

We will go into greater depths on the elements individually to give you a better view on how to work with each one, and offer sample spells that harness the energies of these essential building blocks of the universe.

Earth

The element of earth, our Mother, the Goddess, the giver of life. She is stable, everlasting, eternal and from where all life springs.

The earth has provided everything we have needed for survival through our entire existence. Food, shelter, clothing, heat (for fire needs earth for its existence), are all necessary for human life to sustain and proliferate itself.

While in the modern age of today, technology smoothes the way for easier living than our ancestors. Though still, the earth provides so much of our existence, we cannot live without her. We walk on solid ground every day; our homes are built from wood given by trees; and our food comes from the nurturing of the earth.

This endless existence of earth lends itself to the properties of the element. It represents stability, foundations, wisdom, strength, and growth.

Often the element of earth is used in prosperity and fertility magic, visualizing an abundance growing from the earth into your life.

Tools associated with the Earth are salt, crystals or stones and, most obviously, the pentacle.

When setting up an altar, you want to have all the elements represented for a traditional layout. The pentacle would be placed in the north, as that is the direction with which earth is associated. The season associated with Earth is winter, with its innate nature of hibernation and protection (often, the Earth Goddess is depicted as the Mother in this time, caring for her newborn baby.) Similar to how we behave during the colder months of the year, nurturing and turning introspective in our lives.

The astrological signs associated with Earth are Taurus, Virgo and Capricorn.

People born under these signs tend to be "grounded" and stable. They are hard workers, though have a tendency for narrow-minded, rigid thinking. Because the Earth symbolizes the eternal, that which lasts forever, Earth signs have a rock solid mentality that serves them well. They can however reveal to be challenging when dealing with a more volatile sign.

Colors associated with the Earth are green, brown, black and white.

When working with the element, it is a wise choice to have these colors about you. Wearing earth colors can give you a sense of being grounded, and working with candles in the earth colors can help increase the power of your intent in the craft.

Earth energy, while stable, flows in cycles and can be disruptive in terms of earthquakes, or other natural phenomena. Those who are prone to Earth energy can feel a sense of "uprooting" when things in their life change, such as moving or finding a new job.

If you describe someone as stubborn or inflexible, they are often emitting Earth energies and, when you recognize that in a person, you can learn how to work or communicate with them more effectively.

To connect with the element of earth, you can do simple things such as walk outside barefoot in the dirt and grass, plant a flower in a pot, using your bare hands to manipulate the soil, or even prepare a meal, thinking about the origins of each ingredient, as they came from the earth before reaching your kitchen.

Doing any of these will not only bring you closer to the element, they will help you build a stronger relationship with the divine.

Air

The very element we breathe in, air is our most basic human need. Without it, we cannot exist. Simple as that.

All the elements rely and relate to one another. Air is an ever moving and active element, bringing new ways of looking at old situations. It fuels fire and helps support all forms of life, just like earth.

When we speak, we use air to carry our words and sounds forward. We take a deep breath, expanding our lungs, and our exhalations feed the plant life which surrounds us.

Because of its expansive quality, it explains the nature of air and the personality it presents. Air rules intellect and the astral plane. Air energy helps us communicate as well as gaining fresh perspectives on things that have become stagnant or dormant in our life.

It is an element perfect for reaching the recesses of the mind, moving forward, and learning.

Spring is the season of air, quite literally because, after the long, cold winter, it is literally a "breath of fresh air" to get outside again.

Tools associated with air are incense and the feather, promoting creation energy, free flowing and always moving.

Gemini, Aquarius, and Libra are the astrological signs associated with Air. People born under these signs tend to have a sense of detachment that can serve them well when seeing the bigger picture. With their bird's eye view of the situation, they see potential ideas, thoughts, abstract thinking that most do not.

Just as Earth energies are grounded, Air energies have their home in the clouds. It is an ethereal element, one in which people who have Air energy do not stay in one place for very long. It is a powerful element, aiding in inventive thought processes and keen awareness of intellect.

Connecting with Air energies can be as simple as smelling a fragrant flower in bloom, as scents are associated with the element as well.

If you have the opportunity, hike up a small mountain or even a hill. On a windy day, it is an exhilarating feeling, having the air whip around you, almost as if it will carry you away.

Air is an element of freedom and travel as well, and perfect to call upon for a safe journey. In calling the quarters when you cast your circle for performing rituals or any kind of magic, Air resides in the East. When you set up your altar, you should keep your incense and feather in the east corner.

Working with air can open the mind, help with answers and ideas, as well as divination and astral projection.

Keep an open heart and an open mind when asking the elements for assistance. They flow through you and work with your own energies.

Fire

The element of Fire, powerful and warming, destructive and creative, inspiring love and fear. It is perhaps one of the most popular elements associated with magic, and essential to post-Cro-Magnon life. As humans have evolved over the millennia, the use and control over fire has been a defining aspect of our history.

Fire is transformative, and it represents change within and without us.

For fire to exist, it must consume earth and air, yet it has a creative power that allows us to metamorphose into our ideal self or situations. Fire sheds light in the dark and, just like the sun brings in a new day, the element of fire ushers in the change needed when we feel lost or uncertain.

It is perhaps the most dangerous of the elements. Where you can immerse yourself in earth, air or water, fire can kill you if you plunge yourself into it. Yet it is captivating and to watch and hear it can be quite hypnotic.

Tools for the craft that are associated with Fire are the athame and candles.

The corresponding direction of Fire is south; that is why you should place your athame in the south corner of your altar. It is a masculine element, and rules anger as well as lust. It is a veritable force, stubborn and strong. Fire is excellent for banishing or getting rid of unwanted obstacles, inciting change.

Aries, Leo and Sagittarius are the astrological signs associated with Fire.

People born under these signs are typically leaders, commanding attention. They are courageous and enthusiastic, as well as stubborn and often forthright. Honesty is essential to the Fire signs, just as flames burn away all fogginess to see clearly, truthfully. To know a Fire sign is to love them and be drawn to them for their charismatic personalities, just as the moth is drawn to the flame.

Working with Fire can be dangerous and also exhilarating. It is best to ensure safety of the area and people when working with fire, no matter if it is a small tea light to be lit, or a massive bonfire.

To attune with Fire's energies, you can sit in the sun, absorbing his rays of warmth and light, or even dance to tap into the rhythmic vitality of this element.

Fire brings about transformation and change. When you feel yourself stuck, or unhappily trudging through life, look to Fire to light your path. You will be ready to burn a path to success, utilizing the power of motivation, leadership, and movement that Fire offers.

In Sabbat celebrations, Fire is often a key part of rituals. Whether dancing around a bonfire, or lighting the bale-fire to consume all negativity, it is an incredibly powerful energy with which to work.

Using Fire in sex magic can bring an explosive union that would rival that of Shakti and Shiva.

Water

Water is all around us, inside us, required for existence. Shape-shifting, nourishing, soothing, cleansing. Without water, nothing living can exist on Earth. Our physical composition is made up of mostly water and we can go only a few days without it before serious health risks.

Water is flexible, existing in three different physical states: solid, liquid, and gas.

It has destructive capabilities such as floods and hurricanes (in combination with wind and earth); it can extinguish fire and also cleanse. The scent of a summer day just after a rain storm is clean and full of earth's bountiful aromas.

Despite its destructive capabilities, water is an element of love. The feeling of love washes over us when we are with friends and family. Water is a healing element, feminine in nature and corresponds with the West.

Tools used to represent water are the chalice and cauldron.

This also represents the womb, fertility and feminine energies. Place your chalice in the west corner of your altar for a traditional layout. Also, the season of autumn is associated with the element.

Water can be used in divination, using it to scry on a bowl or cauldron. For best results, use a dark colored bowl, and be patient. If you are accustomed to meditation, this mental state will serve you well to see the answer to your question in the water.

The astrological signs associated with water are Pisces, Cancer and Scorpio. The personality traits of people born unto these signs are often the most psychic of all the signs. They tend to feel and understand human emotions better than others.

People who carry water energies are great healers and counselors. They are excellent listeners and can empathize easily with others. Being comfortable with their own emotions make Water energy people excellent artists. They are able to tap into the right side of their brain very easily.

Negatively, Water energy can be overemotional and difficult to handle. Just like stagnant ponds, water can become lethargic and unhealthy. Often, Earth energy can boost the Water element into action, just as Fire can shine his light into Water's dark recesses.

When working with the element of Water, it is best used for healing and love spells. To connect with the element, simply have a glass of water, keeping mindful awareness of where the water comes from, how it nourishes and keeps you hydrated.

Go to a stream, river, lake or ocean and observe the power of water. Feel the expanding love in your heart when you do.

As with any element, be grateful for Water's cleansing and healing powers. Feel its heaviness, pulling away all the negativity surrounding you, and feel thankful for its regenerative force.

Not only can water help you connect with the divine, but it will bring you closer to yourself through reflection.

The Fifth Element: Spirit

The fifth element, called Spirit by Wiccans, or Akasha which means "space" in Sanskrit, is the divine essence in all things. It is the collective conscious of everything that exists in the universe as it is the source of all energy.

The Greeks added this element to the Four Classical elements, calling it aether, meaning pure air or sky.

Spirit is intangible and is the conductor for all energy, powering all magickal rituals. It is all four elements in equal balance, the infinite thread that connects everything. There are no astrological correspondences, and no tools that represent Spirit because it encompasses all. It is north, south, east, west, down, up, sideways, leftways and in every direction.

Ancient Hindu philosophy included the fifth element as well, though they referred to it as sound or vibration.

To connect with Spirit, slowly chant the word "Om" in a rhythmic pattern. Though we cannot see or hear the Spirit like we can Water or Fire, we can still sense it.

Because Spirit is the divine being and it encapsulates everything around us, we may never fully understand it with our limited mental capacity to grasp such abstract thought. We are always evolving and stretching the limits of the human mind; remember science is merely magick that can be explained!

Until the time comes where we can wrap our minds around the concept of Spirit, of the divine, and all the other mysteries of energy work, keep practicing. Know that with each step you take in your magickal journey, you are getting closer to knowledge.

Now that you have a better understanding of the elements, you can see easily how each one can help you in your spellcrafting.

Once your intent is defined, choose the element or elements that are most appropriate to assist you in your ritual.

Elementals

Without going into great detail, I would feel remiss if I did not explain elementals, in case you encountered them without knowing what they are.

They are in fact nature spirits, who have no defined form, but who belong to the four Classical elements. They are volatile and can be mischievous, which is why we always want to be respectful of the elements.

They are watched over by the Guardians of the Watchtowers, so it is essential to use proper wording as to not inadvertently invite the elementals into your circle. While they can be very helpful, they can also wreak havoc. Even for an experienced witch, they can be problematic. Always treat them with kindness and reverence!

- **Gnomes**, the elementals of Earth, can bring confidence and steadfastness to a witch when called upon. In folklore, they inhabited the caves in the Earth, protecting their hidden treasures. If a witch befriended one, they can be extremely loyal and helpful. Quite the reverse if you angered one;

- **Sylphs** are associated with Air and can bestow creativity and inspire even the most dreadful poet to write a beautiful sonnet. They can be the gentle breeze on your face and just as easily become the whipping dangerous wind that brings down trees. If you listen closely, you can hear them speaking in the wind;

- **Salamanders**, representing the element of Fire, are the most powerful of the elementals – being able to expand or contract in size as needed. They are also the most mischievous and, like children, do not understand the consequences of their actions. They have the power to influence the minds and decisions of the people around them;

- **Undines or nymphs**, inhabit the element of Water. Not only regular water but any kind of moisture, humidity, even vapor. They are very emotional creatures and can influence a person's emotions. They are very open to aiding people in their magickal or mundane workings.

The reason I bring these beings up is because it can be confusing when doing your own research. I want to make sure you are being very clear on the benefits and drawbacks of working with elementals. While all great witches work with the elements, there are few who work with the more volatile beings.

If you encounter an elemental in your work, just be respectful and thank them for their help. Do not banish them. It would create more problems than you could imagine!

To get your feet wet working with the elements, here is one of my favorite exercises, kind of like a spiritual pick-me-up.

I relate closely to Fire, and whether you do too or have a different element to which you are in sync with, this spell is simple and effective.

To perform it, you will need:

- A glass of red wine;

- Cinnamon;

- A red or white candle;

- A chalice or wine glass.

And here's how to proceed:

1. Sit comfortably at a table and pour the wine into your chalice or glass;
2. Sprinkle a little cinnamon into the wine and stir with your finger;
3. Light the candle and spend a minute or two watching the flame and clearing your mind;
4. Hold the chalice in your hand and repeat these words while watching the flame:

"Flame of warmth, flame of light

Fill me with your fire so bright

As I will, so mote it be!"

5. Drink the wine, feeling the warmth spread through your body;
6. Let the candle burn down and feel the fire burn within you.

Chapter III: Casting Circles

There are so many ways and philosophies on how to cast a proper circle... Not to mention when a circle is needed (if it is ever) or if any spells should be cast without one.

<u>Here is my recommendation</u>: read as much as you can, garner as many different viewpoints as possible, and choose whichever one feels right to you or take from several different ritual types and create your own.

The Purpose of Circles

Casting a circle is an important step in any kind of spellcrafting because **it protects the magick from unwanted energy**. I do not cast a circle for every spell I work; however, for important ones where I will be using a lot of energy, or if it is a tricky spell, I never go without one.

Back when I cast my first circle, I held note cards in one hand and used my finger to point where I wanted the circle. It was slow and deliberate, and I was constantly worried about saying the right things. I was so nervous!

What I can tell you now, in hindsight, is: do not worry!

You will make mistakes. You will inadvertently say the wrong thing. And you know what? It is totally okay! It will not make you any less of a great witch. Why? Because your *intent* is what matters. Let the words flow naturally. Understand what each step in casting a circle means, and it won't matter what you say or what you do. You will be successful.

There are a few crucial parts in casting a circle:

- Visualizing the circle as a bubble (its existence is not just on one plane);

- As above, so below. You need to respect the boundaries, not just in a psychological manner, but physical too;

- When you cross a cast circle, you break the holding and containment power of it. Remember that this includes furry friends too!

- Believe in the circle, its strength and the ability to keep unwanted energies out;

- Lastly, have confidence in what you are doing. Like I said, it's okay if you jumble the words or make a mistake. Your intent is still there and will help reinforce the circle's energy. I may be exaggerating but you could say almost any words you want and, as long as you are confident, act with intent and follow the visualization rule, the circle would be cast properly.

Magick Exercise V – Create Your First Circle

The first step in casting a circle is simply to be mindful of the space you are choosing to perform your ritual in.

Make sure you won't be interrupted by family, friends (furry or otherwise), technology and so on. And make sure you aren't under time constraints, not to have to rush things.

Collect any supplies you will need for your spell and your altar (if you are not casting it around your actual fixed altar) and place them in the area of your circle.

Sometimes, making a checklist can help, as you do not want to forget anything and have to cut a door to exit and reenter your circle. Your checklist can be the beginning entry in your Book of Shadows for this particular ritual. It will also help you stay focused and organized.

Choose a tool to use for casting your circle, such as an athame or wand. You can also use your hand or finger to point the boundary of your circle.

Begin in the East, walking clockwise (deosil) and travel your circle using your tool to point at the floor where your circle will be.

Say these words as you walk:

"I walk this circle for the Elements,

that which makes up everything in the universe."

Once you complete one complete circle, begin again walking deosil and say these words:

"I walk this circle for Self,

that which connects to the divine."

Walk a third time around your circle and say:

"I walk this circle for Spirit,

that which connects all living things."

After you have passed East a third time, step into the center of your circle to call the quarters.

I like to think of this step as having your own Secret Service detail. The quarters are the Elements, the Guardians of the Watchtowers in each direction. Seek their aid in protecting the circle from any negative energies, and protect you from harm. Speak to them with due respect, and always thank them when you are finished.

Turn facing the East with your hands up above your head, palms up. Close your eyes or keep them open, your choice and say the following:

"Hail to the Guardians of the Watchtowers in the East, element of Air.

I ask for your aid and protection to watch over this rite

and grace us with truth within it."

Now, face the South with your arms raised above your head and say:

"Hail to the Guardians of the Watchtowers in the South, element of Fire.

I ask for your aid and protection to watch over this rite

and grace us with love within it."

Next, face the West, again with your arms raised and say:

"Hail to the Guardians of the Watchtowers in the West, element of Water.

I ask for your aid and protection to watch over this rite

and grace us with cleansing tides within it."

Lastly, turn towards the North, arms raised and say:

"Hail to the Guardians of the Watchtowers in the North, element of Earth.

I ask for your aid and protection to watch over this rite

and grace us with wisdom within it."

Your circle is now cast!

Visualize a bubble, a full circle that extends above your head and below ground in a perfect round shape. If you need to leave the circle for any reason, use your tool to cut open a doorway, cutting in the opposite direction (counterclockwise or widdershins), and reseal it after to pass through it.

Repeat the procedure when you come back, ensuring you reseal the doorway properly. This will keep your circle intact and free of unwanted energies.

How to Release a Circle

Now, to open or release your circle, you will do the same actions you did to create the circle but in reverse. Begin with thanking each of the Guardians of the Watchtowers, from North going widdershins to East.

Say the following at each quarter:

"Thank you, Guardians of the North (West, South, East),

Element of Earth (Water, Fire, Air) for blessing my circle.

May you depart in peace with my deepest gratitude. Blessed Be."

Walk three times around the circle, going widdershins.

When complete, kneel down with palms on the ground. This act is known as grounding the energy. With all the magic you just performed, the energies need a place to go. Sending them back into the Earth is like recycling them back from whence they came.

As mentioned in the beginning, be sure to read as many variations on casting circles as you can to find the one that is perfect for you. If this is it, great!

Practice casting a circle, recording your experiences in your Book of Shadows. As you practice, you will build your confidence and experience up until this act becomes second nature.

Chapter IV: Sabbats

The Sabbats are so much fun to celebrate because they coincide with nature's wondrous events. Living in New England, it is a perfect pagan cycle of living with nature and celebrating all her changes throughout the year.

If you live in a climate such as southern California, this by no means should inhibit you from celebrating the Sabbats! There are holidays in every religion, all beautiful and worth celebrating in their own right.

We will only be covering the pagan ones in this section.

February 1: Imbolc

This is the start of the growing season, originally dedicated to Brighid, the goddess of fertility. It is mentioned in the earliest of Irish literature, and today has become St. Brighid's Day in Christianity. Another name for it is Candlemas, celebrating the Goddess' transition from Crone to Maiden (two faces of the Triple Goddess, Maiden-Mother-Crone.)

Imbolc is halfway between the winter solstice and the spring equinox. The end of winter is near and we begin to shake off the cold weather and snow. In some ways, it is like coming out of hibernation, and to begin planning the new growing season.

It is a celebration of the coming of light, spring, and new beginnings. Celebrate with candles, bonfires, or any kind of natural light. It is a time for cleansing, like cleaning in preparation for spring. However, do not limit this activity to your home; ensure that you also purify your spiritual house.

Winter was a time of reflection, and now it is time to dust off the past and look to the future, and choose what seeds you want to grow this year.

It is also a good time to perform a recleansing and reconsecration of your tools.

March 20/21st: Ostara (Spring Equinox)

Ostara marks the beginning of spring, and probably sounds very familiar, like another holiday you have heard of called "Easter".

The roots of the Christian holiday were borrowed from the pagan one, marking the young Sun God's mating with the Maiden, who will give birth becoming the Mother again in nine months. It is symbolized by the egg and the rabbit, figures we now associate with Easter.

Rebirth, just like resurrection, begins in the spring. Now is the time for planting. Ostara is a day of fertility and rebirth. If you live in northern climates, it is best to begin planting seeds indoors at this time. And sowing your gardens if you happen to be located in more southern climates. Not only do we plant physical seeds for food and beauty, but spiritual seeds as well.

We plan what goals we want to nurture through the next four Sabbats, ending with full harvest.

Here is an excellent spell to work at this time of year, which will help you increase your power over the season. It is one of my favorite spells, which I still perform every year at Ostara.

For this spell, you can do it one of two ways:

- You can purchase a small flower pot, some potting soil and some plant seeds;

- Or you can just plan to sow your spell straight into the ground in your yard or a spot you often visit.

You will need a pen and paper to write what it is that you want to increase or manifest. Love is a wonderful aim for this.

If you want to grow love into your life, write down as specifically as possible what you want. An example would be:

"Bring love into my life

One that will grow and stand the test of time.

Love that will light the flame of passion

Starting as a sprout and growing for years to come.

May it harm none, as I will, so mote it be!"

Fold your paper up and place it in the bottom of your flower pot. Top with potting soil and plant your seeds into the pot. Care and nurture for your seeds as they

grow into sprouts and on to blossoms.

What I love about this ritual is that the plant serves as a constant reminder for you to focus on your goal.

Remember, you must act in harmony with what you want to manifest. If you want love in your life, make room for it. If you are a workaholic and have no time to have a love life, you aren't welcoming love into your life. Got it?

Try sleeping on one side of the bed. Make space in your closet for another person's belongings. Make time in your schedule for social events. Act as though you were already receiving what you want, and the universe will deliver.

This is a major aspect of harnessing your natural power, to act in accordance with your desires and flow with the will of the universe.

May 1st: Beltane

Beltane, beginning on the eve of May 1st, also known as May Day, honors the living or life in general.

In the old Celtic ways, it was the time of year to light the bonfires and run the herds through the "belfires", promoting good health and fertility.

Being the last of the spring fertility Sabbats, it is celebrated with bonfires and watching the seeds planted at Ostara begin to sprout. Celebrations often begin at

sunset on April 30th and continue through until sunrise on May 1st. It marks the start of summer, the reawakening of the earth, with trees and flowers beginning to blossom.

By celebrating with bonfires, symbolizing the sun's warmth and light, we honor the divine to keep the young crops safe from late frosts or other factors that could harm the harvest throughout the season.

Beltane is one of the most joyous of the Sabbats. Music and dancing are all part of the Beltane rituals, and making your own May Pole can be a great way to celebrate it.

June 20/21st: Litha (Summer Solstice)

The summer solstice is a magnificent Sabbat, celebrating the longest day and shortest night of the year. It marks the turning of the Wheel from light to dark, waxing to waning.

The growing season turns into the harvest season. In ancient times, it was a fire festival celebrated with torch-lit processions, lasting all night and day, the fires fueling the sun's power.

The Goddess becomes Mother, giving birth to the Holly King, who will be with us through the harvest and colder months. The Oak King is gone, and the Mother will slowly become the Crone aspect of the Triple Goddess.

The best way to celebrate is to enjoy a day in nature,

reveling in her beauty in the summer season. Connecting to the divine is as easy as spending some quiet time listening to the birds singing, the rustling of the trees and, where possible, the purr of a river flowing or waves splashing on the beach.

Have a noontime picnic, include some form of fire, and celebrate the warmth of the summer. Create a crown out of freshly picked flowers, reveling in all of nature's beauty and bounty.

Revisit the seeds you planted at Ostara. How are they growing? Are you nurturing them regularly? What further actions can you take to ensure a good harvest of those spiritual seeds?

August 1st: Lughnasa (Lammas)

In mythological lore, the Celtic God Lugh transfers his power to the grain, making it grow strong and bountiful. He sacrifices himself at the harvest in order that he may feed his people, helping them live through the winter. Sounds familiar?

Summer is in full swing and we begin harvesting the early crops like peas, strawberries, and early grains. The earth is in her full splendor with flowers, greens, and warm weather in abundance.

Now is the time to take stock of what we have planted and what we are going to harvest in the next two Sabbats. What actions have been successful? What have

we gained so far in our journey?

To ensure a bountiful harvest, we must continue nurturing our souls.

Make a loaf of bread, honoring the God Lugh. Be sure to leave a piece for him as an offering for his gifts to us. Any bad habits that have formed this growing season can be placed into a "wicker man" made from sheaves of grain, and then tossed into the bonfire.

September 20/21st: Mabon (Autumn Equinox)

This is when light and dark are equal, and all of nature is in balance. The autumnal equinox is time to celebrate all that has been achieved in the growing season. The second of the harvesting holidays, it is a time of celebration of food.

The crops have mostly been harvested, the fields are turning brown and leaves are changing colors. The warmth of summer is fading and we know the harsh winter lies ahead.

Reap the benefits of your spiritual growth and begin to store your harvest to sustain you through the winter.

We mourn the Sun God, thanking him for all that he has given us. It is a chance for us to reflect on not only the past season, but our lives as well. What good things have you manifested in your life?

Mother Nature is turning to her darker side, and she is

represented by the mother, soon to become the crone. What wisdom have you gained? What good habits have you formed that you will take with you into the winter months?

Celebrate Mabon by writing in your journal, and creating a feast to share with your friends and family.

October 31st: Samhain

My most favorite Sabbat of all! Obviously coinciding with Halloween, which is primarily a children's holiday borrowed from the pagans. Costumes are so much fun to incorporate into any celebration. Samhain, pronounced "sow-en", honors our ancestors and the dead.

It is the final harvest, where what we have reaped is what will last us through the winter. No more actions can be taken to grow and foster our plants that are now dying in the fields. Mother becomes the crone, the old wise woman. We honor our ancestors by thanking them for all the wisdom they have bestowed upon us.

The veil between the worlds of the living and the dead is always thinner at the major Sabbats, but perhaps the thinnest at Samhain.

One way of celebrating it is to prepare a large meal to share with friends and family. An extra plate is set at the table to represent those who have come before us. Fill it with food, in expectation of the spirits of your ancestors who will join you.

Once the meal is complete, put another plate on your doorstep. The essence of the food will be consumed by passing spirits. It is an honoring of the dead, and serves as protection for your home on this night.

If you find an empty plate in the morning, not only have you fed the spirits, but maybe some fairies as well! It is considered the pagan New Year's Eve, as everything has died and we are headed into the darkest of days until the winter solstice.

Samhain is also the perfect time for banishing the unwanted things in your life. This spell can be done with other witches or "muggles" alike. I have many friends and family who have their own spiritual path but still enjoy this activity every Samhain.

If you have a cauldron (preferably cast iron) or any other fireproof material, this is the perfect time to use it. If not, use something that can contain a flame safely, as you will be burning paper in it.

You will need individual pieces of paper and pens for everyone, and a lit candle with which you will set the paper aflame.

Explain to each person that you want to write down what you wish to banish, and be sure to include the rule of three!!!

For example, if you wanted to banish your boss from

your life, and you wrote "I want to banish my boss from my life", this could result in you losing your job. Be smart in the wording!

Say you wanted to banish negative energy and thoughts. Here is how it would best be written:

"I want to banish all negative energy from my home

and negative thoughts from my mind.

May this spell harm none. So mote it be!"

This will protect you and your home from any potential karmic backlash.

Once everyone has their banishment written out, have them fold it up and do not share what each person wrote. This weakens the power of the spell.

Take turns lighting the paper from the candle and dropping it into the cauldron. Watch the flames as they burn and go out on their own.

When the cauldron has cooled, carry it outside and toss the ashes on the wind to be carried out to the universe.

Always remember: act in accordance with your wishes and the power will grow and manifest even faster.

The longest night of the year, where we find ourselves surrounded by the cold. Our bountiful harvest gets us through the difficult months, sustaining us until spring.

The Goddess becomes the Mother again, giving birth to the Oak King, who will bring us light, warmth and spring.

Yule is the last of the holidays of the calendar year. Light will be growing each day going forward. It is a time to celebrate the light with candles, candles, and more candles.

Like all the other fire festivals, we use the flame to power the sun. While the other celebrations are more outdoor, public rituals, Yule is a domestic, home at the hearth type of ritual.

A fire in the hearth and a good meal from our earlier harvests are excellent ways to welcome in the light. Yule logs, never bought but given or found in the woods are decorated with evergreens and burned all night long in the fireplace. Letting it smolder for as long as possible, to help bring in the light.

We know spring is coming, and we will have more light with each passing day. The giving of presents is a wonderful way to celebrate this holiday, sharing your bountiful harvest.

To practice and expand your power, choose the next Sabbat and begin planning a celebration for it. If it is in a few days, just keep it simple but, if you have a couple of weeks, make it as involved as you can, beginning with a ritual and end with a feast!

Chapter V: Pantheons

I have mentioned quite a bit about the God and Goddess, but we haven't really covered pantheons or the many faces of those Gods and Goddesses. First, let me explain to you how I view the Divine as a whole, and perhaps it will all make a little more sense as we delve deeper into various pantheons.

Conceptualizing the Divine

The human mind has a limited capacity for understanding. We can only explain what we can see, read, hear or experience.

To say "I know God" is to be in touch with the Divine within oneself, because no one has actually seen God, nor can anyone truly conceptualize God. How can anyone be so arrogant as to say they can grasp an entity so massive, all knowing, powerful, and omniscient?

They simply cannot.

And that's not an insult; it's just a fact. However, all witches view the Great Horned God and the Triple Goddess as two parts of the same whole Divine entity. Imagine the string of energy that connects all things coming from one large energy source. This is the God and Goddess.

They have several faces, He being the Oak King, bringer of light and the Holly King, the bringer of darkness. She has three faces: Maiden, Mother and Crone, or the three stages of a woman's life. Both give life, and love us unconditionally. To believe in them, is to believe in yourself.

Now, here's where it can get tricky.

When casting a spell, we may not need the all-powerful Mother Goddess, just a piece of her. But how rude of us to invite just a part of the most amazing Divine being in existence to help us in our little spellwork? Instead, we call upon the divinity we need. If we are doing a protection spell for our home, for example, we may call upon Brighid, the Celtic Goddess of home and hearth, healing, and smith-work.

Do you see where we are headed here?

When in need, we may feel more comfortable calling upon diverse pantheons to which we are connected rather than the all-powerful God or Goddess. Being an eclectic pagan myself, I chose from several different pantheons; however, I feel closest to the Celtic and Greek pantheons.

I use the word "chose" lightly. It is only partially a witch's choice whom they work with as you are often called by a deity into their service as well. It can be a mutual decision, or completely one sided. The most important thing you can do is keep an open mind. You may love a deity in one pantheon, and then dislike the rest of them.

I know of some great witches who choose to work only with Egyptian Gods and Goddesses, and others who work solely with the Norse pantheon. It is merely preference. But one thing remains the same across the pantheons:

The Gods and Goddesses from each pantheon represent just a facet of the much larger Divine being whom we choose to call the God and Goddess.

Like the facets of a diamond, the pantheons we work with are just small fractions of the larger whole. Makes sense? Maybe a pie chart will help.

The Divine Entity - God and Goddess

Conceptualizing the Pantheons

The entire circle represents the Divine entity, balanced as male and female, the God and Goddess. I chose four of the Celtic Gods and Goddesses to show that they make up the whole and that they represent a part of the God and Goddess – yes, only one part of them.

I know, trying to understand the scope of the Creators of all living things can seem daunting, but if it is put into a human perspective, sometimes that is all that is needed to grasp the idea.

So, now that you have a better grasp of the role of the God and Goddess, let's look at the pantheons.

Working with one or more pantheons serves as a deeper connection to the Divine for every great witch. It is also a very personal connection, as some pantheons will attract you and others will repel you.

For me, I do not work at all with the Egyptian pantheon because, for some unknown reason, I feel like it is evil. I have absolutely zero basis for this thinking, but I have felt this way for as long as I can remember. And the first rule is to trust your gut, remember?

Conversely, I am very attracted to the Celtic pantheon, more than likely due to my Irish lineage. The Greek pantheon is also one that I am drawn to, for my love of the mythology I grew up reading about. It isn't out of the question for me to tap a Norse Goddess or Hindu God, depending on my intent and purpose.

Choose what feels right to you, and keep your mind open. That is all there is to know.

I will introduce some of the major pantheons, but I highly encourage you to research more. You may find one that resonates with you unlike any other, or perhaps you will take a few from each pantheon that you encounter.

There is no wrong way to connect to the Divine.

The Greek Pantheon

The Greek Gods and Goddesses are probably the most well-known, thanks to Greek mythology being part of many higher education curricula. There are eight classes of Immortals in the Greek pantheon:

- The first group, the Protogenoi, were the first; literally the Genesis of all things. They are simply named, Gaia who is Earth; Pontos, the Sea; Ouranos, the heavens, etc;

- The second group are the spirits and nymphs, which includes the dryads, satyrs, and tritones;

- The third class represented body and mind affecting spirits, such as Phobos (fear), Eros (love), and Hypnos (Sleep);

- The fourth class is the Immortals who controlled the forces of nature. In this group, you will find the Titans such as Kronos. If you read the Percy

Jackson series, you will be very familiar with the Titans, as well as...

- The fifth class of Immortals: the twelve who rule from Mount Olympus. These are the ones we will discuss most;

- The sixth class is the constellations, including the twelve Zodiacs. Sagittarius was the centaur Chiron, or Kheiron for example;

- The seventh class contains the monsters and beasts, such as giants, centaurs and sirens;

- Lastly, the eighth class is for the demi-God heroes like Perseus, Theseus and Achilles.

Going back to the twelve who rule from Olympus, known as the Olympians... they are the class that correlates with other Gods and Goddess in other pantheons.

You will always find the counterpart in another pantheon, so if for some reason you aren't connecting well with Aphrodite, the Greek Goddess of Love, perhaps Venus, the Roman Goddess of Love will suit you better. Or Aine (pronounced Awn-ya), the Celtic Goddess of Love may resonate more deeply with you.

Zeus, the King of the Gods, Father of Men, represents Law & Order, Justice, and his realm is of course, the sky. If you are working a spell and need karmic justice or protection, Zeus is a powerful God that can help and add power to your intent.

Hestia, the Goddess of the Hearth is a wonderful kitchen helper. I call on her when I am making dinner and looking for a little Divine inspiration. She is very handy in all domestic tasks, and keeping a peaceful, loving home.

Apollo, the Greek God of medicine, poetry, art, and archery, is a wonderful God to call upon for healing spells, especially when using the power of the sun or flame in your spell.

Dionysus is perhaps one of my favorite Gods, the God of winemaking, wine, theater, and religious ecstasy. He is a wonderful God to conjure for Sabbat celebrations, especially Beltane.

There are many more Greek gods, enough to take up a whole series of books!

So, if you are intrigued or feel a pull of attraction, I would definitely recommend researching them further.

The Hindu Pantheon

Hinduism is said to be the oldest religion in the world. It is by far the most complex and organized of all the religions with a hierarchy of gods and goddesses, merely facets of one eternal, infinite being.

Contrary to popular belief, Hindus do not worship many gods, as Hinduism encompasses traits of both polytheism and monotheism, and is often referred to as kathenotheism (the belief of one individual god of a group, each taking a turn.)

You do not have to be a believer of Hinduism in order to call on its gods and goddesses. The energy is there, ready for you to call upon for help. As there are many names, manifestations, and the overall hierarchy to understand, I won't go into great detail with exception to Shiva and Shakti.

Shiva, the god of destruction and spouse of Shakti, is often misunderstood by non-Hindus. When we think of destruction, we think endings, sadness, pain and suffering; however, everything that has a beginning, has an end and truly is not an "end" but part of a transformation.

Shiva represents the destruction of ego, of transforming oneself into a higher creation, closer to the divine. He is the patron of yogis and represents the inward journey to finding oneself.

He and Shakti form the perfect complement of man and woman. Their love is so strong and powerful, at one point it even frightened the other gods. Shiva being the destroyer and Shakti the ultimate nurturer and mother perform together in such a way that keeps the balance in the cosmos, and here on Earth.

Shiva is often considered ambiguous because of his role as a celibate yogi and that of lover/husband to Shakti.

While he can be seen depicted as a god in meditation, pure in mind, body and soul, he is also an intense lover and father to his family, providing two aspects in which one can worship.

Shiva can be called upon for several purposes, and to truly connect with him, you must get to know him. He is helpful in getting rid of bad habits or ending something to make way for a new, better path.

One of the best ways to commune with Shiva is to invite him to join you in meditation. Also, inviting him and his beloved Shakti to preside over marriage ceremonies (a common Hindu practice in all marriages) is a wonderful way to bless a sacred union.

The union of Shiva and Shakti is the most powerful of all the gods at your disposal, and perhaps in any pantheon. While apart, they are two separate gods; together they are one, and from them all things are created. They are the ultimate power couple, representing the infinite cycle of birth, destruction, and rebirth.

Being polar opposites, when they collide in their primordial union, it is an expansive and electric force of energy. When choosing to work with them, be aware that energy juice they will give you is extremely powerful, and certainly not for the beginner.

Shakti, as we have discussed, is the wife and lover of Shiva. She embodies the mother goddess, for without their Shakti, all the gods would be powerless. For every god, they have an equal and opposing goddess, the source of their power. She is the divine, everlasting energy of creation.

Shakti is the ultimate creative energy, the eternal feminine who can assume the form of mother and wife as easily as young maiden and a whore. She is the sexual energy within all women, the fertile mother, and the wise old sage. Shakti is equivalent to the Triple Goddess in paganism. It could be their roots are from the same source...

To invite Shakti into your ritual, you must be prepared for some serious power. She is not one to consort with in a lighthearted fashion. She is truly all powerful, and can be extremely helpful in spells of love, fertility and any type of creativity.

A wonderful activity to commune with Shakti is to go into the woods, or any place you feel connected to the goddess, and sit quietly. Breathe with the earth and slowly chant the words "Adi Shakti, Namo Namo". This is a Kundalini chant, essentially meaning "I bow to the primal energy."

Using these two powerful entities can lead to very intense spellcrafting. There are plenty of other Hindu gods and goddesses to work with also, if this pantheon speaks to you.

Like the Greek pantheon, the Celtic is steeped in mythology, arguably as old as the Greeks as well. While there are the eight classes of Gods in the Greek pantheon, the hierarchy of Gods in Hinduism, there is no specific classification in Celtic lore except for regions.

You will find different names for the same gods and goddesses in different parts of Ireland and Great Britain as a whole.

Some of the Celtic deities can be found as far as the Gallic Empire reached. The Celts had a major influence in religious beliefs, which can explain the pagan deity similarities in Western and Northern Europe.

Some of the most popular Celtic Gods conveniently became Catholic saints. It helped ease the pagans into Christianity by having familiar names and holidays for them to relate to.

We mentioned Brighid earlier, and she has many spellings to her name from Brigid, Brigit, to Brid. She is seen as three sisters, all very different aspects from healing to smith-work to poetry. Brighid is the daughter of the Dagda, a powerful God, father figure and protector of the tribe. She is also one of the Tuatha de Danann, a supernatural race in Irish mythology.

Brighid is the perfect Goddess when performing any kind of healing spell. She will help guide your hand to good health for yourself or whomever you are helping. I find Brighid to also be helpful in inspiring creativity, especially in writing.

Cernunnos is one of the more well-known Celtic Gods, known as the Horned One. He reflects the Wheel of the Year, birth, death and rebirth of all things. He is a hunter, a masculine energy and is very helpful in spells to increase power, love, or abundance.

Aine is the quintessential Goddess of love, sovereignty, wealth, summer and fertility. She is an abundant Goddess, celebrated at the Midsummer Sabbat, Litha. She can give or take away power, just as she can give or take away love. She is a wonderful Goddess to use in fertility and love spells.

The Morrigan (Great Queen) is another important goddess to know in the Celtic pantheon, as she is the goddess of sovereignty, battle and strife. She is represented by the crow and is often depicted as the Crone version of the Triple Goddess, but is often depicted as three sisters.

She can be very helpful, when shown due respect, especially in matters regarding military or political in nature.

Discovering Your Pantheon

The deities we invoke, or request aid from are incredibly helpful. Before you go calling Brighid of the Celtic pantheon to join you in a spell, you will have to get to know them first.

If you needed help fixing your sink, would you go outside your front door, call to the first stranger, asking them to come in and help you?

It is highly rude to the Divine to expect aid from them when you don't even know them.

It is so important to do proper research in deciding which deities and pantheons will work best for you and your magick. There is a long list of pantheons from around the world and whether you choose to go by heritage, colorful history, or just because you like their names, making the decision should not be made lightly. And you may find that a god or goddess calls upon you while doing your research.

The list of gods and goddesses within the pantheons is extensive. Listed below are some pantheons for you to research. Write them down in your journal and pick one or two a day to research.

To avoid overloading and confusion, keep it to just one or two per day.

List of Pantheons:

- Celtic;

- Norse ;

- Hindu;

- Egyptian;

- Welsh;

- Scottish;

- Greek;

- Roman;

- African;

- Japanese;

- Mayan;

- Native American;

- Slavic;

- Incan;

- Germanic;

- Chinese.

Side note: There is a theory that the pantheons we are attracted to generally relate to our past lives. For example, where I am completely repelled by the Egyptian pantheon, something may have happened to me in a past life that is related to Egypt, Egyptian deities, or even the Middle East as a whole.

This holds true for other things in our lives that we love or feel an affinity to; there just isn't hard evidence to back up the theory. Just some food for thought...

Conclusion: Practice Makes the Witch

The path to awaken the witch within and harness the power you hold inside is a long journey that can be the most beautiful, eye-opening adventure you will take in your life.

Learning to use spells and dealing with higher powers can be both overwhelming and exhilarating. Even after 22 years of practicing the craft, I am still learning and still get giddy with excitement after a powerful spellcrafting session.

Now, with all the information I shared with you in this guide, you should have the basics needed to begin your journey and growing your power. As with everything worth your while, it will take practice and experience before you reach greatness.

I said in the beginning that magick is merely science unexplained. To find the truths for yourself, you need to conduct many experiments (spellcrafting), record your results (Book of Shadows), continue building your confidence and strengthening your intent.

It was once considered magick to predict the weather. In ancient times, there were soothsayers and fortune tellers who merely had an aptitude for awareness of patterns and their surroundings. It seemed like magick, where today we know it is just meteorology.

Our human minds cannot grasp the scope of the Divine;

therefore, it is not a big leap to know that there is still magick, things we do not have a name or explanation for yet. Working with the elements, in tune with nature and all living things, brings us closer to the truth, and the Divine.

Alchemy was considered a type of magick, going back four millennia. Yet, one very notable alchemist was Sir Isaac Newton, one of the world's most celebrated scientific minds. While alchemy is more of a scientific philosophy, the experiments were considered mystical until our understanding caught up with the magick and it became science.

So, becoming a great witch now could mean you are at the forefront of scientific exploration. You could be the next millennium's Isaac Newton!

Just like the thread connecting all living things, the steps in this book are all interconnected:

- Following the Sabbats connects you to the rhythm of nature;

- Keeping a record, your Book of Shadows, brings you closer to yourself, while building confidence in each step you take;

- Your tools and working with the deities help strengthen your intent.

Once you see the interconnectedness of the journey, you

will find yourself well on your way to becoming a powerful witch. The power is within you, waiting to be tapped!

In this first volume, I have given you various spells and wordings for cleanings, consecration, circle casting and many other spellworking. I am sharing with you the words I use to perform these spells, and I collected them through my 22 years of experience, research, trial and error.

Use what feels right to you. Change the words, or use the ones you read in other books. It does not matter, only the intent does.

Speaking of other readings...

Have you ever heard the expression, "don't believe everything you read"? This phrase is doubly true for the Internet! There are some very good sites, informative and handy. Witchvox is a great place to visit for some research, as well as Christopher Penczak's website.

When you read something, do your best to verify it from multiple sources, and do lots of research. It is better to have a well-rounded view of something than just take one person's word for it.

There are many books out there on paganism, witchcraft, and variants of the nature based religions. Pick a few from different authors, and maybe sprinkle a little Buddhism or Native American works in there as well.

Read anything you can get your hands on. It will help you further connect with the divine as well as arm you with knowledge from many perspectives. When studying history, you wouldn't read just one book on the Civil War for a complete understanding because it could be written from only one side's point of view, right? If you read "Gone with the Wind", you would have a distinct southern slant to your view on the Civil War.

Aside from reading and doing your own research, practice writing some of your own spells. Start small, like a Sabbat celebration or a protection blessing on your beloved family pet and work your way up to the bigger stuff as you gain confidence.

Remember, this is your path to walk, no one else's, there are no wrong ways to do something.

Keep the Rede in mind at all times as your guiding beacon. Karma will always have her revenge, so you don't need to do her job. The Rede also applies to casting spells on or for others without their knowledge. In the world of witchcraft, casting a spell on an unsuspecting friend is akin to invading someone's home.

I am sure your intentions are well meant, but you do need someone's permission to cast a spell on them or on their behalf. Imagine the spell as ketchup. You wouldn't want someone throwing ketchup on you unless you said it was okay, right? Yes, I am intentionally being silly but only to make a point.

It is imperative that even the most well intended healing spell for your very sick friend be done with their permission in order to avoid any kind of karmic kickback.

It will also make your spells more powerful because then your friend can act in accordance with the spell, thereby flowing with the energy you are sending them. Makes sense?

You have the power, knowledge, and now the tools to harness your natural power. It is up to you to take the first step in becoming a great witch. Enjoy the journey and may our paths cross again soon!

Excerpt from Book II

To give you an idea of things to come once you've mastered your basics, here is an excerpt from my next book in the *How to Become a Great Witch* series:

"Once you have your crystals, you need to cleanse them before you perform any magick. It is very easy and also necessary. When crystals touch any other living being or something that has been imbibed with energy, it absorbs and holds it. You never know what type of energy you will come across when you first receive your crystal. Whether it is one you personally dug out of the ground or purchased from a reputable source, the crystal contains energy.

The earth is where they are formed, and it will be more natural energy from occurrences like earthquakes, rain, or even the little worm that squiggled across it. When you purchase a crystal, it may have passed through many hands before reaching yours.

There are many ways to cleanse a crystal, and you just need to be aware what methods are best for the crystal you have chosen.

Moonlight/Sunlight cleansing is a wonderful and easy way to purify the energy in your crystal. Moonlight is best for amethyst, as sun will cause it to fade. Sunlight works great with quartz crystal. Whichever method you choose, place your gem in direct line of the moon/sun.

Don't worry if it is cloudy or overcast weather, the rays will still penetrate your crystal and cleanse it. For both moonlight and sunlight, 24 hours of direct contact should be sufficient. If you are working with a stone to banish negativity such as rose quartz, citrine or black tourmaline, leave it out in your chosen light for at least 48 hours.

There is no limit to how long they can sit in the light for purification, so if you are going away or forget that you set out crystals for purification, nothing bad will come of it.

Salt is another method of cleansing, but there are some crystals who deteriorate with contact. Using salt water is a very quick and thorough method of cleansing your gems, however there are many that have adverse reactions to it because they are porous, contain water or metal. It can even change their composition.

You can reference in a quick Google search, or you can avoid it and just go with a method that does not require contact with salt. Take a bowl and fill it 2/3's of the way up with salt, preferably sea salt. Choose a smaller bowl that will fit inside and place it so it is submersed halfway up in the salt. Put your crystal in the smaller bowl, so it is not making contact with the sea salt.

Pour a little bit of purified or moon water into the smaller bowl, just enough to cover the crystal. The salt will purify the stone, absorbing all the energy in it while the water protects the stone from any drifting salt crystals. Leave your gem in the water for a few days.

Once your gem is cleansed, remove it and dry it with a natural cloth such as cotton or silk and throw away the salt, as it holds all the energy from the crystal it absorbed.

Earth is a wonderful purifier, as that is where the crystals are formed. For this method, you will need a natural fiber bag and a trowel or something with which to dig and scoop. Find a nice patch of earth, free from chemicals or pesticides, and dig up enough to fill a medium size bowl. Scoop the earth into your natural fiber bag and take it home.

Choose a bowl that will hold the earth and empty your bag. Place the crystals directly into the earth. Let them rest in the earth for 5-7 days.

When the crystals are cleansed, dust them off with a natural cloth, and deposit the earth back from where it came. Bring a little bit of water with you and pour it over the earth used in the cleansing and thank Mother Earth for her energies.

Cleansing should be repeated as needed. For example, if you use a stone in a particular spell and want to use it in a new spell with a different intent or purpose, re-cleanse the crystal. Also, if it is one that helps repel negativity or transforms negative energy into positive, it will need to be cleansed every week or two. You will know when the time is right, by sensing the energy within the crystal.

To emphasize the necessity of cleansing your crystals, the story of the Hope Diamond is one with an impressive and dark history. While some facts are not certain, what we do know is in 1668 a French merchant named Jean Baptiste Tavernier stole a large diamond from the temple of Rama in India. In retribution for the thievery, the priests charged the stone with negative energy, essentially cursing the diamond.

The diamond, known as the Tavernier Blue, French Blue, and eventually the Hope Diamond was sold to King Louis XIV. Marie Antoinette frequently wore it, including it in her collection of the royal jewels. The diamond was stolen in 1792 during the French Revolution and the French Blue as it was known then was never seen again. It resurfaced in 1839 when Thomas Henry Hope acquired it.

This is where the Hope diamond we know today got its name. It was not officially confirmed until 2005, when a 3-dimensional lead model of the French Blue was found in the archives of the French Natural History Museum. It became clear the Hope Diamond was cut from this beautiful stone. What makes the Hope Diamond unique is the color it turns when under ultraviolet infrared light. The Hope Diamond and her sister stones derived from the original French Blue are the only blue diamonds to glow red hot under infrared, which only fuels the theory of the curse placed on it by the priests.

It is said that anyone who comes in contact with the

stone will be touched by the curse. Jean Baptiste Tavernier was mauled by a pack of wild dogs. Jacques Colet who purchased the stone in the early 1900's committed suicide. Prince Ivan Kanitovski, who bought it from Colet, was killed in the Russian Revolution.

Mademoiselle Ladue, who borrowed the stone, was supposedly murdered by her lover. Simone Menicharides, who possessed the diamond briefly, was thrown from a cliff. Abu Sabir who was commissioned to clean the stone was imprisoned and tortured. Kulub Bey, a guard of the stone, was hanged by a mob in Turkey. Nicholas Fouquet who reportedly wore it once was disgraced and died in prison.

While the history of the curse of the Hope Diamond is a nefarious tale, there are nuggets of truth to every legend. The lesson to be learned is **always cleanse your crystals**!

Now that your gems are cleansed, it is time to empower them.

We took away the energies it collected, and now we are going to give it our own energy to help us in spell work. You want to get familiar with your crystal, and vice versa. Choose a quiet space, and hold your crystal in your receiving hand (non-dominant hand) and observe the colors, striations, shape, size and visual properties.

Close your eyes and send out psychic feelers to the crystal, like little white energy filled fingers from your mind, sensing the make-up of the crystal. Let the gem speak to you. Keeping your eyes closed, gather energy into a small white ball in the center of your chest. Hold it there, letting it gain more power, getting brighter with more energy.

When you have a lovely white ball of swirling energy, visualize it traveling down to your dominant hand ("projecting" hand). Place your projecting hand over the crystal and release the energy from your hand into the crystal.

You have just empowered your crystal. It has your energy now, and will respond to what you want the crystal to do for you.

Crystals and Protection

With all the negative energy that can pervade our beautiful world, with the help of crystals, you can keep from dragging it around with you, into your home and your sacred spaces. Negative energy can come from an infinite number of sources; even electricity has negative energy in it (electrons).

The more natural occurring energy such as electricity, storms, plus the man-made negative energy such as cell phone signals, radio waves/antennas can permeate our life to the point where we feel heavy. Utilizing crystals perfect structure and ability to absorb energy make them ideal for protection.

Crystals can also be used in the protection of your home, car, business, children, pets and of course, yourself. Just like with any purpose, there are crystals whose properties suit us best for defense.

Some common examples include:

Black Tourmaline: it is best for deflecting negative energy directed at you, for example psychic attacks. If you plan to attend a large pagan event such as a festival or ritual, it is recommended to have a black tourmaline with you, fully charged for defending against anyone trying to play psychic vampire and take your energy.

Amber: this one is a good choice for getting rid of negative energies. When moving into a new home or new office, placing a piece of amber by the doorway will help neutralize any incoming negative energy.

Quartz: here's one stone that is excellent for protecting your home from negative energy and those who wish you ill. Bury four pointed quartz in the four corners of your property, points facing away from your home. These will act as deflectors or transmute incoming energy from negative to positive.

Smoky Quartz: you want protection in the workplace from other people's stress? Place a smoky quartz on your desk, charging it to keep a bubble around your area and everyone's stress away from you.

Fluorite Stones: these are perfect for concentration and focus, with a side benefit of transforming negative energy into positive. Keep a charged fluorite handy on your desk where you study or work, and you will stay productive.

Green Aventurine: it acts as a shield to protect your energy, especially emotional energy from your heart. Keep one on your person to ensure your energy is kept inside you!

You will note, as we delve deeper into the understanding of the extensive uses of crystals, that some of the same types of crystals pop up for different uses.

Crystals have individual properties as well as their own electromagnetic vibration. The intent is the trigger to tap the vibrations, so the crystal will work in harmony with your goal.

For instance, the lodestone is a magnetic stone, drawing what you want to you. It can be used for a variety of purposes such as power, healing, attraction (of anything), friendship and love, fidelity, business and money to name a few. It can be confusing, with all the different uses for just one stone. However, using lodestone in combination with rose quartz would be a powerful way to project intent on your gemstones, by attracting love to you.

Protection is important in the magickal world, as energy is constantly flowing all around, through and inside us. Practice focusing your intent for protection will help you master it, thereby keeping harm at arm's length.

Here is a simple spell for protection, one to keep on your person...

You will need:

- A small black tourmaline;

- Cloves;

- Salt;

- A teaspoon of olive oil;

- A small vial/bottle that fits in your purse or pocket.

Bring all your items to your sacred space, and place them together. With your projecting hand hovering over the items, close your eyes and think thoughts of protection, such as a white ball of light surrounding the items.

Once they are charged with the power of protection, place the salt, tourmaline, and cloves in the vial. Top off with the teaspoon of olive oil.

Seal the bottle tightly and hold it in your hands. Visualize the white energy inside the vial growing to envelope you, creating a bubble. Keep the vial with you, recharging it once a week.

If you are feeling nervous or entering a situation where

you do not feel comfortable, just shake the vial for a super surge of protection."

As you can see, crystal and candle magick (and so much more) will be included in book II of this series. May your journey bring our paths together again in the next volume!

Made in the USA
Monee, IL
02 April 2021